CHAT GPT CASHFLOW

EXPLORING LUCRATIVE WAYS TO MAKE MONEY WITH CONVERSATIONAL AI

ABBIX PUBLISHING COMPANY

Contents

1. Introduction to AI and ChatGPT 5
1.1 Understanding Artificial Intelligence 5

2.2 The Rise of ChatGPT 7

1.3 Crafting Irresistible Prompts for Optimal ChatGPT Results 12

2. Crafting Captivating Blogs & Articles using ChatGPT 20
2.1 Choose the Right Keyword 20

2.2 Title Generation 22

2.3 Write the Introduction 25

2.4 Create an Outline 28

2.5 Content Generation 32

2.6 Paraphrasing for Human-Like Touch 38

2.7 Crafting a Compelling Facebook Post and Meta Description 43

3. Other Ways of Monetization with ChatGPT 47
3.1 Using AI to Craft Compelling YouTube Video Script.. 47

3.2 Creating Prompts for the Creation of Text-to-Image . 51

3.3 AI Text-to-Speech for Monetization 54

3.4 Unleash Your Musical Creativity with AI........................56

3.5 Writing Code with ChatGPT to Earn Money 61

3.6 Create a Recipe Blog and Monetize Your Passion for Cooking..66

3.7 Breaking Languages Barriers with ChatGPT 71

3.7 Empowering Your Academic Journey with ChatGPT 72

4. Using ChatGPT to Market Your Business...77

4.1 Crafting Engaging Social Media Posts 77

4.2 Optimizing Email Marketing with ChatGPT..................78

4.3 AI-Generated Blog Post Ideas for SEO 82

5. Bonus Prompts for You to Choose from!...87

5.1 Business ChatGPT Prompts..87

5.2 ChatGPT Prompts for Students...98

5.3 ChatGPT Prompts for Coders..100

5.4 ChatGPT Prompts for Poets...106

5.5 Prompts to Tell ChatGPT to Act Like Someone...........108

5.6 Best ChatGPT Prompts for Writers................................114

5.7 Wining ChatGPT Prompts for Video and Podcast Content..118

Chapter 1.0

Introduction to AI and ChatGPT

1.1 Understanding Artificial Intelligence

Artificial Intelligence (AI) is a technology that emulates human intelligence in machines. By enabling computers to learn from data, make decisions, and execute tasks without constant human input, AI's core concepts encompass "Machine Learning," which allows machines to learn from data, and "Neural Networks," replicating the human brain's structure.

In the real world, AI finds applications in various domains. Personal assistants like Siri and Alexa efficiently assist us with everyday tasks, while healthcare benefits from AI in medical diagnoses and drug research. Self-driving cars and drones skillfully use AI to navigate safely, and finance relies on AI for stock predictions and fraud detection. Moreover, AI chatbots proficiently handle customer inquiries, further enhancing efficiency.

The advantages of AI are substantial. Automating repetitive tasks, significantly increases efficiency, leading to improved productivity. Furthermore, AI's capability to process vast amounts of data enhances decision-making in fields like business and healthcare. Its ability to personalize experiences, ensure safety, and mitigate risks further adds to its appeal.

Nevertheless, AI has its limitations. Due to its lack of emotional understanding and empathy, it falls short of interacting like humans. The presence of bias in

AI can result from biased training data, leading to unfair outcomes. Additionally, the expense of AI implementation makes it less accessible for certain individuals or organizations.

Ethical considerations play a vital role in AI development. The use of extensive data raises privacy concerns, and the potential job displacement caused by AI automation requires careful attention. As a result, developers must approach the design of AI systems ethically, avoiding harm and respecting human values.

AI, as a potent technology with practical applications, demands a comprehensive understanding of its concepts and implications to responsibly harness its potential. As AI continues to advance, addressing ethical concerns becomes essential, ensuring that its benefits are accessible to everyone without discrimination.

2.2 The Rise of ChatGPT

In recent years, there has been a remarkable surge in technological advancements in artificial intelligence (AI). One of the most notable achievements during this period is the emergence of ChatGPT, a language model developed by OpenAI. Utilizing innovative deep-learning techniques, ChatGPT has the remarkable ability to generate human-like text and engage in meaningful conversations with users. In this chapter, we delve into the practical aspects of ChatGPT's rise and its invaluable contributions across various domains.

One practical application of ChatGPT is its integration into customer support services. Numerous companies have leveraged ChatGPT-powered chatbots on their websites to assist customers with common queries and issues. These chatbots are available 24/7, offering instant responses and eliminating the need for customers to wait for human agents. This accessibility ensures a seamless customer experience, leading to increased satisfaction and loyalty.

ChatGPT's proficiency in understanding user preferences and behavior also makes it a fantastic tool for delivering personalized recommendations. Whether it involves suggesting products, movies, or books, ChatGPT can analyze user data and provide tailored recommendations that align with individual tastes. E-commerce platforms, streaming services, and content recommendation engines have eagerly embraced this practical feature.

Moreover, ChatGPT has become a valuable resource in the field of learning and education. Acting as a virtual tutor, it answers questions, explains complex concepts, and offers examples to help students better comprehend various subjects. Additionally, educators can use ChatGPT to create interactive learning materials and quizzes, fostering a more engaging learning experience for students.

https://pixabay.com/illustrations/ai-generated-chatgpt-chatbot-8177861/

For writers and content creators, ChatGPT has emerged as an invaluable writing assistant. It aids in generating ideas, overcoming writer's block, and providing suggestions for enhancing the flow and structure of written content. Many authors and bloggers have seamlessly integrated ChatGPT into their creative process, benefiting from its ability to offer fresh perspectives and novel angles for their work.

ChatGPT's multilingual capabilities have further enhanced its practicality, particularly in language translation. Users can input text in one language and receive accurate translations in real-time, effectively breaking down language barriers and facilitating cross-cultural communication. This feature has proven indispensable for international businesses, travelers, and language enthusiasts alike.

In the world of software development, ChatGPT has found its niche as a coding assistant. Developers can interact with ChatGPT to seek help with coding problems, obtain suggestions for more efficient code implementations, and explore various programming concepts. This practical application saves time and significantly enhances productivity throughout the programming process.

Beyond these applications, ChatGPT has also found a purpose in the mental health sector, providing support and companionship to those in need. Users can engage in conversations with ChatGPT, sharing their thoughts and feelings and receiving empathetic responses. While it is not a substitute for professional therapy, it can offer a temporary source of comfort and encouragement for individuals seeking emotional support.

The rise of ChatGPT has revolutionized our interaction with AI, bringing practical benefits to various aspects of our lives. From improved customer support to personalized recommendations, educational assistance, writing support, language translation, coding help, and even mental health support, ChatGPT has demonstrated its versatility and utility as a valuable tool for users worldwide. As technology continues to advance, we can look forward to even more practical applications of ChatGPT, further enriching our daily experiences.

1.3 Crafting Irresistible Prompts for Optimal ChatGPT Results

In the vast landscape of online opportunities, harnessing the power of ChatGPT to generate income can be a significant change. One of the most critical factors determining your success lies in your ability to formulate prompts that elicit the best results from this AI marvel. In this chapter, we delve into the art and science of crafting prompts that not only optimize your interactions with ChatGPT but also open doors to lucrative online ventures.

1. Understand the Basics:

Before diving into the intricacies of prompt creation, it is essential to grasp the fundamentals. ChatGPT responds to the context you provide in your prompt. Keep your queries concise and to the point. Strive for clarity and precision in your language to help the AI understand your intent accurately.

Example:

Instead of: "**Tell me about marketing strategies.**"

Try: "Provide a brief overview of the latest digital marketing strategies used by successful e-commerce businesses."

2. Context is Key:

To achieve meaningful and relevant responses, it is crucial to provide the AI with the necessary context. Introduce your conversation, establish the persona or role you want the AI to assume, and outline any specific guidelines for the interaction. This foundation will set the stage for a productive dialogue.

Example:

Context-setting: *"Imagine you are a financial advisor. A client is seeking advice on long-term investment options. Provide comprehensive recommendations based on their risk tolerance."*

3. Be Specific:

Vague prompts can lead to ambiguous or off-target responses. Instead, frame your queries with specificity. If you are seeking advice, ask for actionable steps or real-life examples. When seeking creative content, provide details about the theme, tone, and direction you have in mind.

Example:

Specific query: *"List three practical steps individuals can take to reduce their monthly energy consumption and lower utility bills."*

4. Clear Instructions:

Think of ChatGPT as a helpful assistant that needs precise instructions. If you want the AI to generate a list, comparison, or pros and cons, explicitly state your requirements. Use bullet points or numbered lists to organize your instructions effectively.

Example:

Clear instruction: *"Present a comparison between the advantages and disadvantages of hybrid cars versus traditional gasoline-powered cars. Format the information as bullet points for easy readability."*

5. Tone and Style:

Consider the tone and style of the responses you desire. If you are engaging the AI to draft content for a formal business proposal, maintain a professional tone. For casual conversations, adjust your language accordingly. Communicating your desired tone will guide the AI's outputs.

Example:

Tone specification: *"Write a persuasive product description for a new line of sustainable fashion accessories. Maintain an upbeat and eco-friendly tone throughout."*

6. Iterative Approach:

Sometimes, the initial response may not fully meet your expectations. Embrace an iterative process where you provide feedback and guide the AI toward refining its output. This approach nurtures a learning experience for both you and ChatGPT, enhancing the quality of subsequent interactions.

Example:

Iteration feedback: Initial response: *"Provide tips for better time management." After feedback: "Expand on the importance of prioritization in time management and share a personal anecdote to illustrate its effectiveness."*

7. Experiment and Adapt:

Do not be afraid to experiment with different phrasings and structures. Often, small tweaks can lead to significantly improved outcomes. If you are not getting the results you want, try rephrasing your prompt or breaking it down into smaller queries.

Example:

Experimentation: *"Describe the benefits of meditation for mental health." Variant: "Explain how incorporating a daily meditation practice can positively impact individuals' mental well-being."*

8. Avoid Bias and Sensitivity:

ChatGPT is a powerful tool, but it is important to use it responsibly. Avoid prompts that could lead to biased, offensive, or harmful content. Be mindful of the potential consequences of your requests and prioritize ethical considerations.

Example:

Ethical awareness: *"Compose a blog post discussing the challenges faced by underrepresented communities in the tech industry and suggest strategies for fostering diversity and inclusion."*

9. Utilize Examples:

Drawing inspiration from examples can be immensely helpful. Explore pre-existing interactions, review sample prompts, or refer to online resources for guidance. Learning from successful prompt structures can enhance your own abilities.

Example:

Learning from examples: *"Build upon the previous response and create a step-by-step guide for beginners on setting up an e-commerce store, including selecting a niche, choosing products, and setting up a payment gateway."*

10. Practice Patience:

Rome was not built in a day, and neither is a mastery of prompt creation. As you engage with ChatGPT, you will develop an intuition for crafting effective queries over time. Patience and persistence will be your allies in refining your prompt-writing skills.

Example:

Patience in action: *"Ask ChatGPT for recommendations on improving communication skills. If the initial response lacks depth, refine the prompt to specifically request practical exercises and real-life scenarios."*

Remember, the quality of your prompts directly impacts the value you derive from ChatGPT. By mastering the art of prompt creation, you unlock a world of possibilities for using ChatGPT to generate income online and beyond.

Chapter 2.0

Crafting Captivating Blogs & Articles using ChatGPT

2.1 Choose the Right Keyword

The first and most critical step regarding content creation is choosing the right keyword. This determines the focus of your article and helps you target the right audience. Keywords play a vital role in search engine optimization (SEO) as they are the terms users type into search engines when looking for information. Finding the perfect keyword can be challenging, especially if you want to balance moderate competition and good search volume.

Previously, you might have relied on ChatGPT to assist you with keyword research. However, ChatGPT's data is limited to information before September 2021, so it might not be up-to-date with the latest trends and search patterns. Instead, you can turn to tools like Bard AI for keyword research to stay current with the rapidly changing digital landscape.

Bard AI is designed to continuously update its database with the latest search trends and user behavior, ensuring that the keywords it suggests are relevant and aligned with the current interests of your target audience. By prompting Bard AI with the following request:

"Can you suggest a relevant keyword with moderate competition and good search volume for my blog post about [topic]?"

You can gain valuable insights into keywords that will resonate with your readers.

For example, suppose you are planning to write a blog post about *"digital marketing strategies in 2023."* You ask Bard AI for keyword suggestions, and it comes up with *"cutting-edge digital marketing techniques for 2023"* as a suitable keyword. This keyword captures the essence of your content and will likely attract readers interested in the latest marketing trends and strategies for the current year.

With Bard AI, you can feel confident that your content will be optimized for search engines and effectively reach your target audience. By keeping up with the latest keyword trends, you increase your chances of attracting more readers and establishing yourself as a credible source of information in your niche.

So, embrace the power of advanced tools like Bard AI for keyword research and take your content creation to new heights. Remember, staying up-to-date with the latest keyword trends is crucial to creating engaging and successful content in the ever-evolving digital landscape.

2.2 Title Generation

A captivating blog post title can make a significant difference in attracting readers to your content. It is the first impression readers have of your article, and it must be compelling enough to make them click and explore further. Crafting an attention-grabbing title is an art that requires a careful balance of creativity, relevance, and curiosity.

To generate attention-grabbing titles for your blog posts, you can once again turn to the power of AI with ChatGPT. By prompting ChatGPT with the following request: *"Can you create several catchy blog post titles that include the keyword '[keyword]' for my article about [topic]?"*, you will receive a plethora of title ideas that not only incorporate your chosen keyword but also pique the interest of your target audience.

Imagine you are writing an article about "Cutting-edge digital marketing techniques for 2023." You decide to use ChatGPT to help you come up with captivating titles. ChatGPT responds with ideas like:

"Unleashing the Power of Digital Marketing: Top Techniques for 2023"

"Future-Proof Your Business: Implementing the Latest Digital Marketing Strategies in 2023"

"Revolutionizing Your Marketing Game: Discover the Best Techniques for 2023"

"Stay Ahead of the Curve: Mastering 2023's Digital Marketing Innovations"

"From Good to Great: Elevate Your Marketing with 2023's Cutting-Edge Techniques"

"Driving Success in 2023: The Ultimate Guide to Innovative Digital Marketing"

"Digital Domination: Conquer 2023 with These Dynamic Marketing Tactics"

"The Next Era of Marketing: Embrace 2023's Revolutionary Strategies"

"Elevate Your Brand: Embracing the Future of Digital Marketing in 2023"

"Unlocking Success: Your Roadmap to 2023's Top Digital Marketing Tactics"

Each of these titles not only includes the keyword "Cutting-edge digital marketing techniques for 2023" but also adds a unique twist that sparks curiosity and entices readers to learn more. These titles give potential readers a glimpse of the valuable insights and knowledge your article has to offer, making them eager to dive into the content.

With ChatGPT's help, you can now confidently choose the perfect title that aligns with your article's focus and resonates with your target audience. Remember, a compelling title is like a gateway to your content, and by leveraging AI-generated suggestions, you can increase the chances of attracting more readers and gaining a loyal following for your blog. So, experiment with different titles, pick the one that best represents your content, and set the stage for an engaging and informative read.

2.3 Write the Introduction

The introduction of your article or blog post is a crucial element that sets the tone and engages your readers right from the start. A well-crafted introduction serves as a gateway to your content, capturing your audience's attention and motivating them to explore further. It should introduce the topic and establish its relevance and create curiosity, leaving readers eager to delve deeper into your insights.

To create an introduction that effectively accomplishes these goals, you can again turn to ChatGPT's power. By prompting ChatGPT with the following request: *"Can you write an introduction that effectively introduces '[topic]' to '[target audience],' establishes its relevance, and creates curiosity?"* you will receive an engaging and thought-provoking introduction tailored to your article's focus and audience.

Let us consider an example where your article's topic is "cutting-edge digital marketing techniques for 2023," and your target audience is marketing professionals and business owners seeking to enhance their strategies for the coming year. ChatGPT generates an introduction like:

"Are you ready to revolutionize your marketing game and stay ahead of the competition in 2023? Traditional marketing approaches are needed in the ever-evolving digital landscape, where consumer behavior and technology intertwine. As marketing professionals and business owners, embracing innovative strategies is the key to unlocking unprecedented success in the year ahead. In this article, we dive deep into innovative digital marketing techniques for 2023, equipping you with the knowledge and tools to thrive in a fast-paced and dynamic market.

Get ready to embark on a journey that will transform how you approach marketing, unlocking new possibilities and opportunities for your brand."

This introduction effectively introduces the topic of "cutting-edge digital marketing techniques for 2023" to the target audience of marketing professionals and business owners. It establishes the subject's relevance by highlighting the rapidly changing digital landscape and the need for innovative approaches to stay ahead of the competition. The introduction also creates curiosity by hinting at the valuable insights and transformative journey that awaits the readers as they explore the article.

By leveraging ChatGPT's assistance, you can craft introductions that captivate your audience, enticing them to read on and discover your wealth of knowledge. Remember, a compelling introduction sets the stage for an engaging and informative article, paving the way for a rewarding reading experience for your audience. So, experiment with different approaches, find the one that resonates with your audience, and make your articles stand out.

2.4 Create an Outline

An organized and well-structured outline is essential for seamless content creation. It serves as a roadmap, ensuring your article flows smoothly and covers all relevant aspects of your chosen topic. To create a content outline, you can once again rely on the assistance of ChatGPT. Instruct ChatGPT with the following request: *"Can you create an outline with well-structured sections covering different aspects of '[topic]'? Make sure to include subheadings and key points."*

Let us continue with the example of an article on "cutting-edge digital marketing techniques for 2023." ChatGPT generates an outline with well-structured sections as follows:

Outline: Cutting-Edge Digital Marketing Techniques for 2023

1. Introduction

- ➡ Introduce the significance of digital marketing in the modern business landscape.

- Briefly mention the rapid changes in technology and consumer behavior influencing marketing strategies.

- Highlight the importance of adopting cutting-edge techniques to stay competitive in 2023.

2. Social Media Marketing Trends

- Discuss the latest trends in social media marketing for 2023.

Subheading 1: "Influencer Marketing Evolution"

- Key points on how influencer marketing is evolving and shaping brand promotion.

Subheading 2: "Interactive Content Engagement"

- Key points on the rising popularity of interactive content and its impact on audience engagement.

Subheading 3: "Social Commerce Boom"

- Key points on the emergence of social commerce and its potential for driving sales.

3. Artificial Intelligence in Marketing

- Explore the role of Artificial Intelligence (AI) in revolutionizing marketing practices.

Subheading 1: "AI-Powered Personalization"

- Key points on how AI-driven personalization enhances customer experience.

Subheading 2: "Chatbots for Customer Support"

- Key points on the benefits of using AI-powered chatbots for efficient customer support.

Subheading 3: "Predictive Analytics for Data-Driven Insights"

- Key points on how predictive analytics helps in making data-driven marketing decisions.

4. Voice Search Optimization

- Examine the growing significance of voice search in digital marketing.

Subheading 1: "Understanding Voice Search Behavior"

- ➡ Key points on how users interact with voice search and its impact on SEO.

Subheading 2: "Optimizing Content for Voice Queries"

- ➡ Key points on best practices for optimizing content to rank in voice search results.

5. Personalization and Customer Experience

- ➡ Delve into the importance of personalized customer experiences in 2023.

Subheading 1: "Customer Journey Mapping"

- ➡ Key points on how to map customer journeys for personalized interactions.

Subheading 2: "Hyper-Personalization Strategies"

- ➡ Key points on implementing hyper-personalized marketing campaigns.

Subheading 3: "Leveraging User-Generated Content"

- ➡ Key points on utilizing user-generated content for enhancing customer experience.

6. Conclusion

- ➡ Summarize the key takeaways from the article.

- ➡ Emphasize the significance of embracing cutting-edge techniques for digital marketing success in 2023.

- ➡ Encourage readers to implement the discussed strategies to gain a competitive edge.

This well-structured outline covers various aspects of "cutting-edge digital marketing techniques for 2023" and provides a clear framework for writing a comprehensive and cohesive article. Organizing your content this way ensures that your readers can easily follow your ideas and access valuable insights on each subtopic. Leveraging the power of ChatGPT for content outlining allows you to focus more on crafting engaging content while ensuring that your article delivers value to your readers.

2.5 Content Generation

Now that you have your outline, it is time to bring your article to life with comprehensive content.

ChatGPT can be your trusted partner in writing detailed and informative sections for each part of your outline. To initiate content generation, prompt ChatGPT with the following request: "Can you write a comprehensive [words] article about '[subtopic]' related to '[keyword],' including practical tips and examples to engage readers?"

Let us continue with the example of the "**Voice Search Optimization**" section in the article "**Cutting-edge digital marketing techniques for 2023.**" ChatGPT crafts a well-researched and insightful piece as follows:

Article: Voice Search Optimization - Embracing the Future of Digital Marketing in 2023

Voice search is rapidly becoming a prominent aspect of digital marketing, transforming how users interact with search engines and digital devices. As voice-enabled devices like smart speakers, virtual assistants, and smartphones gain popularity, businesses must adapt their SEO strategies to stay relevant and accessible to their target audience. In this article, we delve into the rise of voice search and its impact on SEO. We offer practical tips on optimizing content for voice-enabled devices, with real-world examples of businesses benefiting from voice search optimization.

The Rise of Voice Search

Voice search has seen exponential growth in recent years, driven by advancements in speech recognition technology and the convenience it offers users. People increasingly use voice commands to search for information, perform tasks, and purchase online. By 2023, it is estimated that more than half of all internet searches will be voice-based, making voice search optimization a critical component of any digital marketing strategy.

Impact on SEO

Voice search presents unique challenges for SEO as search queries tend to be more conversational and longer. To rank well in voice search results, businesses must understand user behavior and optimize content accordingly. Traditional keyword-centric SEO approaches must complement natural language and contextually relevant content. Moreover, voice search favors featured snippets and concise answers to user queries, so businesses must focus on creating content that provides direct, concise, and valuable information.

Practical Tips for Voice Search Optimization

1. Conduct Keyword Research for Voice

- ➡ Identify long-tail and conversational keywords that match user voice queries.

- ➡ Use tools like Bard AI to explore emerging voice search trends and phrases.

2. Optimize for Local Voice Searches

- ➡ Capitalize on voice search's local intent by optimizing content for local SEO.

- ➡ Include location-based keywords and phrases to attract nearby customers.

3. Create FAQ Pages and Q&A Content

- ➡ Anticipate user questions and provide concise answers in your content.

- ➡ Structure your content in a Q&A format to match voice search query patterns.

4. Improve Page Load Speed

- ➡ Ensure your website and content load quickly on desktop and mobile devices.

- ➡ Faster load times improve user experience and positively impacts SEO.

Real-World Examples

Let us look at how businesses are successfully implementing voice search optimization:

Example 1: XYZ Electronics

XYZ Electronics, an online electronics retailer, optimized its product descriptions for voice search queries. By using natural language and answering common user questions about their products, they saw a 20% increase in organic traffic from voice searches. Additionally, they optimized their website for local voice searches, attracting more foot traffic to their physical stores.

Example 2: ABC Travel Agency

ABC Travel Agency focuses on creating voice-friendly content for their travel guides. Their travel guides incorporated local landmarks, activities, and events, targeting voice search users seeking information about specific destinations. As a result, their travel guides became popular voice search results, leading to a 15% increase in bookings from voice-driven conversions.

In conclusion, voice search optimization is no longer an optional strategy but is necessary for businesses aiming to thrive in the digital landscape in 2023. By understanding the rise of voice search, its impact on SEO, and implementing practical tips with real-world examples, businesses can position themselves for success and effectively engage their audience in this new digital marketing era.

With ChatGPT's help, you can craft detailed and informative content that captivates your readers and offers them valuable insights into the innovative digital marketing techniques of 2023. Remember to provide practical tips and real-world examples to make your article more engaging and relatable to your target audience.

2.6 Paraphrasing for Human-Like Touch

Paraphrasing the content generated by ChatGPT involves rephrasing the text while retaining its original meaning. Here is a step-by-step guide to paraphrasing effectively:

1. **Understand the Content:** Read and comprehend the text generated by ChatGPT to ensure you grasp its core message and key points.

2. **Identify Key Ideas:** Identify the main ideas, concepts, and arguments presented in the original text.

3. **Use Synonyms and Rewording:** Replace words and phrases with synonyms or alternative expressions. Be cautious to keep the meaning of the text the same.

4. **Restructure Sentences:** Rearrange the sentence structure. Change the order of clauses, phrases, or words to present the same information differently.

5. **Change Sentence Forms:** Transform sentences from active to passive voice, or vice versa. Convert statements into questions or vice versa.

6. **Alter Word Forms:** Change the forms of words (e.g., nouns to verbs) or use different tenses to convey the same message.

7. **Add Introductory Phrases or Transitions:** Insert new introductory phrases, transitional words, or connectors to lead into or connect ideas.

8. **Focus on Core Meaning:** Ensure the revised text maintains the original intent and meaning. The paraphrased version should convey the same information as the original.

9. **Check Grammar and Clarity:** Review the paraphrased content for grammatical correctness and clarity. Ensure that the reworded text flows smoothly.

10. **Compare with Original:** Compare your paraphrased text with the original content to ensure you have not inadvertently changed the meaning.

11. **Use Online Tools (Optional):** There are online paraphrasing tools available that can assist in generating alternative versions of the text. However, be cautious, as these tools might only sometimes produce accurate or contextually appropriate results.

The following are the tools that you can use to paraphrase/rephrase the content:

- **QuillBot** is a popular paraphrasing tool that uses AI to rephrase text naturally. It offers a variety of features, including different paraphrasing modes, a grammar checker, and a plagiarism checker.

- **Paraphraser.io** is another powerful paraphrasing tool that uses AI to generate high-quality, original text. It offers a variety of features, including a thesaurus, a synonym finder, and a grammar checker.

- **Cliche Finder** is a great tool for finding and removing clichés from your writing. It also offers a variety of other features, such as a thesaurus, a synonym finder, and a grammar checker.

- **Grammarly** is a popular grammar checker that can also be used to paraphrase text. It offers a variety of features, including a spell checker, a grammar checker, and a style checker.

- **Hemingway Editor** is a great tool for improving the readability of your writing. It highlights areas of your text that are difficult to read and offers suggestions for improvement.

12. **Cite Your Sources (If Applicable):** If paraphrasing content from another source (including ChatGPT), ensure you still give proper credit and attribution.

Remember that while paraphrasing is a valuable skill, it is vital to maintain the integrity of the original content and avoid misrepresenting the author's ideas.

To maintain authenticity and ensure that your content sounds more human-like and engaging, it is crucial to use paraphrasing. By rephrasing the previous section on "Voice Search Optimization," we can achieve a more natural and conversational tone while preserving the accuracy of the information.

Original Section:

"Voice search is rapidly becoming a prominent aspect of digital marketing, transforming how users interact with search engines and digital devices. As voice-enabled devices like smart speakers, virtual assistants, and smartphones gain popularity, businesses must adapt their SEO strategies to stay relevant and accessible to their target audience. In this article, we delve into the rise of voice search and its impact on SEO. We offer practical tips on optimizing content for voice-enabled devices, complete with real-world examples of businesses benefiting from voice search optimization."

Paraphrased Section:

"The use of voice search is growing significantly in digital marketing, revolutionizing how people interact with search engines and digital gadgets. With smart speakers, virtual assistants, and smartphones embracing voice technology, businesses must adjust their SEO tactics to stay relevant and effectively reach their target audience. In this article, we explore the increasing popularity of voice search and its influence on SEO and provide practical suggestions for optimizing content for voice-enabled devices. Additionally, we showcase real-world success stories of businesses that have benefited from implementing voice search optimization strategies."

By employing paraphrasing techniques, we create a more approachable and conversational tone in the content while retaining information and critical points. This way, your article reads as if it were written by a human, ensuring that your audience can seamlessly connect with the insights and advice you provide. Remember, paraphrasing to enhance your content's natural flow is essential in making your AI-generated content appear human-like and authentic.

2.7 Crafting a Compelling Facebook Post and Meta Description

Effective marketing elements for your article are crucial for **promotion and SEO optimization.** ChatGPT can help you create a captivating Facebook post and an SEO-friendly meta description. Prompt ChatGPT with the following requests:

"Can you create a captivating Facebook post for the article titled "[title]," providing a glimpse of what readers can learn?"

Facebook Post:

"Stay ahead of the marketing game in 2023 with the latest trends!

Discover innovative digital marketing techniques that will revolutionize your business! We have gotten you covered, from AI-powered marketing strategies to dominating voice search optimization!

Unlock success in the dynamic digital landscape with our in-depth article on "Cutting-Edge Digital Marketing Techniques for 2023."

Read now and gain a competitive edge! [Link to the Article]

In this Facebook post, we have used an enthusiastic tone to create excitement and intrigue. The post provides a glimpse of the valuable insights' readers can expect from the article, teasing the topics of AI-powered marketing and voice search optimization. By using a call-to-action (CTA) and hashtags, we encourage readers to click the link and engage with the content.

"Can you write a meta description that entices readers to click while incorporating the focus keyword "[keyword]" for search engine optimization?"

Meta Description:

"Discover the top digital marketing techniques for 2023 - AI, voice search, and more to boost your business! Stay ahead of the competition with insights on AI-powered marketing and voice search optimization. Get ready to revolutionize your marketing approach!"

We have crafted a concise and enticing snippet for the meta description that incorporates the focus keyword "digital marketing techniques for 2023." The description promises valuable information on AI-powered marketing and voice search optimization, enticing readers to click and read the full article. Hashtags are used strategically to improve visibility and SEO optimization.

By using ChatGPT's assistance, you can create attention-grabbing marketing elements that effectively promote your article and optimize it for search engines. These captivating Facebook posts and SEO-friendly meta descriptions will entice your audience and encourage them to explore your article's valuable insights. Remember to customize the post and meta description to fit the specifics of your article's content and target audience.

https://pixabay.com/illustrations/finger-touch-hand-structure-769300/

Chapter 3.0

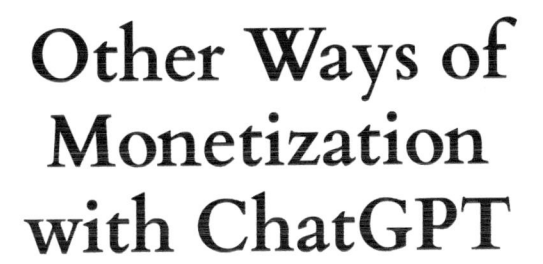

Other Ways of Monetization with ChatGPT

3.1 Using AI to Craft Compelling YouTube Video Script

Are you an aspiring content creator looking to streamline your scriptwriting process? Look no further! In this chapter, we will take you through the art of crafting compelling scripts for your YouTube videos using the power of AI, specifically ChatGPT. By the end of this guide, you will have the tools and techniques to create engaging and well-structured scripts that captivate your audience.

Step 1: Creating an Outline

The foundation of any great script is a well-organized outline. Begin by identifying the topic of your video. Let us say you are interested in NBA legends and their first games. To get started, use ChatGPT with the following prompt:

Can you provide me with guidance and direction on creating an outline for a script that will highlight the initial experiences of (TEXT)?

ChatGPT will assist you by providing a structured outline. However, remember not to solely rely on AI; it is important to add your personal touch and knowledge to enhance the quality of your script.

Step 2: Expanding the Outline

Now that you have a solid outline, it is time to add depth to your script. Use **Perplexity.ai** to expand on each point in a storytelling manner, ensuring your content is engaging. Here is a sample prompt:

"Now provide more details about (TEXT) and make it more engaging and in the best format.

Perplexity.ai will help you elaborate on each point, weaving an engaging narrative that keeps your viewers hooked.

Step 3: Refining Your Script

Once your script is expanded, it is crucial to refine your wording for clarity and coherence. Utilize Grammarly or ChatGPT to polish your content. For example:

"Can you help me improve the wording of this section (Expanded Script) to make it sound more engaging and friendlier?"

These tools will suggest enhancements that maintain your voice while ensuring your script is error-free and impactful.

Step 4: Crafting an Intriguing Hook

Capturing your audience's attention from the start is essential. Use ChatGPT to create a compelling hook by summarizing your script in an engaging way. For instance:

"Can you summarize the script in a way that grabs viewers' attention and entices them to watch the whole video?"

This will help you craft a captivating introduction that leaves your audience eager for more.

Step 5: Transitioning and Concluding

Smooth transitions between sections are key to keeping your viewers engaged. Ensure your script flows seamlessly by asking ChatGPT to suggest effective transition sentences. For instance:

"Now help me create smooth transitions between each section of the (script)."

Lastly, leverage ChatGPT to assist in concluding your video, encouraging viewers to watch more of your content or take a specific action.

3.2 Creating Prompts for the Creation of Text-to-Image

Embark on a captivating journey where the fusion of human creativity and AI innovation intertwines, ushering us into an era of unprecedented possibilities. Join us as we delve into the realm where two remarkable AI entities, ChatGPT and Leonardo AI, come together to redefine the art of scriptwriting.

Welcome to a world where the dynamic duo of ChatGPT and Leonardo AI takes the stage. ChatGPT, the expert in words, and Leonardo AI, the visionary creator of images, unite their powers to elevate scriptwriting to new heights. In a harmonious symphony of text and visuals, they bring your ideas to life in ways that will leave you awestruck.

Step into the world of prompt generation for Leonardo AI. If you are eager to create prompts for Leonardo AI, the journey begins with ChatGPT. Just beckoned,

"Hello, ChatGPT, I want to generate images using AI. Can you provide me a detailed prompt so that AI generates the best image, I want to generate images about (Your Thoughts)?" Add these words in the prompt Hd, HDR, 4K, High quality, Best quality, and more.

Watch as GPT responds, delivering a treasure trove of prompts that you can then feed to Leonardo AI.

Now that you have successfully generated prompts for Leonardo AI, it is time to bring your visions to life. Open Leonardo AI and paste the prompts that you crafted using ChatGPT. As you hit that generate button, watch in awe as Leonardo AI transforms your textual prompts into stunning visual masterpieces.

With your Leonardo AI-generated images ready to dazzle the world, the next step is to turn them into a source of income. Selling your creations is simpler than you might think. Freelance platforms like **Upwork**,

Fiverr, and Freelancer await your talents. Create a captivating profile, highlighting your unique AI-enhanced offerings, and set the stage for a successful venture.

Crafting a captivating freelance profile is paramount. Utilize ChatGPT's prowess to pen a compelling profile description that highlights the innovative blend of human creativity and AI technology. Describe your journey, your passion, and the remarkable potential of your Leonardo AI-generated artworks. Stand out in the freelance marketplace with a profile that beckons clients to explore your visionary world.

As we conclude this journey, the path ahead is radiant with possibilities. From crafting prompts with GPT to generating striking images with Leonardo AI, and ultimately displaying and selling your creations on freelance platforms, your venture into AI-enhanced creativity is destined for success. The tapestry you weave is a testament to the limitless boundaries of innovation. Embrace the future, where human ingenuity and AI brilliance unite, and the world of creative expression knows no bounds.

3.3 AI Text-to-Speech for Monetization

Discover a straightforward process for producing engaging text-to-speech videos using ClipChamp, a user-friendly video editing tool. Ideal for platforms like YouTube, TikTok, and social media, these videos offer a fresh way to share content. Follow these steps:

1. **Sign Up:** Create a free ClipChamp account using your Microsoft, Google, or email credentials.

2. **Initiate Creation:** Access the ClipChamp start page and click *"Create a video."*

3. **Text-to-Speech**: Within the main interface, choose *"Record and create"* on the left. Click the *"text-to-speech"* option. Select your preferred language and voice from a variety of options.

4. **Customize**: Input your text and use punctuation (periods, commas, ellipses, question marks) to adjust speech rhythm and pitch.

5. **Save:** Save your creation to the media bin.

6. **Add to Timeline**: Easily integrate the audio into your timeline by clicking the plus icon or dragging and dropping.

7. **Enhance:** Leverage ClipChamp's video editing features to complement your text-to-speech audio with visuals, music, and more.

8. **Export:** Click *"Export,"* choose your desired resolution (1080P recommended), and ClipChamp will generate an MP4 file with synchronized video and audio.

You are interested in selling your services on freelance platforms like Fiverr or Upwork. Right? Leverage your newly acquired expertise to offer unique and engaging content creation services. Display your portfolio, highlight your ability to customize text-to-speech for various niches, and set competitive pricing. Freelance platforms provide an avenue to monetize your creativity and technical skills, reaching clients seeking captivating videos for their diverse projects.

Elevate Your YouTube Channel: Take your text-to-speech creations to the next level by incorporating them into your YouTube channel. Use these videos for narration, storytelling, or introductions to enhance your video content. Whether you are a vlogger, educator, or entertainer, text-to-speech can lend a professional and distinctive touch to your channel. Embed the audio seamlessly, pair it with relevant visuals, and engage your audience with a unique auditory experience.

3.4 Unleash Your Musical Creativity with AI

Are you ready to infuse your music with the magic of AI? In this easy-to-follow guide, we will explore four exciting AI tools that can take your music to new heights. Whether you are a seasoned musician or just starting out, these tools offer fresh inspiration and innovation. Let us get started!

https://pixabay.com/illustrations/cheers-pleasure-poor-community-204742/

Step 1: Transform Text into Music with Stable Diffusion

1. Get Started: Go online and find a Stable Diffusion tool.

2. Type a Prompt: Write something like "Bongos on a havanistry."

3. Hear the Magic: Listen as AI turns your words into a unique musical piece.

4. Customize Your Sound: Tweak the settings to make it your own.

5. Use in Your Music: Download the audio and add it to your music software. Mix, match, and create!

Step 2: Discover Unique Sounds through Source Sampling

1. Find a Source Sampling Tool: Look for platforms like "Samplelet.io."

2. Set Your Preferences: Choose the genre, views, or country you want.

3. Explore Hidden Gems: Let AI dig up lesser-known tracks for you.

4. Play with Your Finds: Download and slice up these tracks to make them your own.

Step 3: Explore Music with Web ChatGPT

1. Access the Tool: Use a Web ChatGPT with internet access.

2. Ask Questions: Quiz the AI about music theory, history, or anything else.

3. Get Quick Summaries: Receive summarized info from the AI.

4. Apply Insights: Use what you learn to add depth to your compositions.

Step 4: Craft Lyrics with Lyric Studio

1. Find Lyric Studio: Locate an AI lyric generator like "Lyric Studio."

2. Give a Theme: Input a topic like "love" or "adventure."

3. Grab Lyrics: Let AI suggest lyrics based on your theme.

4. Compose with AI: Mix AI-generated lines into your lyrics for a fresh twist.

Step 5: Create MIDI with Muse Tree (Bonus)

1. Access Muse Tree: If available, find Muse Tree or a similar tool.

2. Choose Style: Pick a musical style and instruments you like.

3. Request MIDI: Ask AI to create a MIDI sequence for you.

4. Shape Your Sound: Download the MIDI, refine it, and bring it into your music software.

Step 6: Reflect on AI's Role in Music

As you experiment with these tools, remember that AI is here to enhance your creativity, not replace it. Embrace AI as a sidekick that helps you explore uncharted musical territories.

Now, go ahead and blend AI with your musical vision. With these tools, you have the power to create a symphony of sounds that is uniquely yours. Let us make music that pushes boundaries and captures hearts!

3.5 Writing Code with ChatGPT to Earn Money

Coding is not everyone's cup of tea, we all know. But now, as every industry is revolutionized, coding has also taken a 360-degree shift. With AI assistance, coding has become less hectic. So, in this chapter, you will learn the basics of using ChatGPT to assist you in writing code. Whether you are new to programming or looking for some coding help, ChatGPT can be a valuable tool. Let us get started!

Step 1: Set the Context

Before you start, make sure to provide context to ChatGPT about the programming language, framework, or problem you are working on. This will help the model generate relevant and accurate code examples.

Step 2: State Your Goal

Clearly state what you want to achieve with your code. Are you trying to solve a specific problem, create a function, or implement a certain feature? The more specific you are, the better assistance you will receive.

Step 3: Begin the Interaction

Start your interaction with ChatGPT by introducing your goal and asking for guidance. You can use prompts like:

"I'm trying to write a Python function that calculates the factorial of a number. Can you help me?"

"I'm working on a web development project using HTML and CSS. Could you provide an example of how to create a centered div element?"

Step 4: Ask for Code Snippets

Ask ChatGPT for code snippets, explanations, or pseudo-code to help you achieve your goal. Be as specific as possible about what you are looking for. For example:

"Could you provide me with a Python code snippet that calculates the factorial of a number using a loop?"

"Can you help me write a SQL query that retrieves all users from the 'users' table where the age is above 18?"

Step 5: Refine and Discuss

Review the code snippets provided by ChatGPT. If something is unclear or needs adjustments, ask for further clarification or modifications. You can also discuss the code's logic or potential improvements:

"The code looks good, but I'm not sure I understand how the loop works. Could you explain it in simpler terms?"

"This SQL query is helpful, but what if I also want to sort the results alphabetically by name?"

Step 6: Iterate as Needed

If the initial code snippet does not fully meet your needs, do not hesitate to iterate. Ask for modifications, alternative approaches, or additional code examples until you are satisfied with the result:

"The code you provided works, but is there a more efficient way to solve this problem?"

"What if I want to add error handling to the Python code you gave me? How would I do that?"

Step 7: Express Gratitude

Once you have received the help you needed, be sure to express your gratitude to ChatGPT for its assistance. It is always nice to maintain a positive and respectful interaction.

Example Interactions:

1. Python Factorial Function

You: "I'm trying to write a Python function that calculates the factorial of a number. Can you help me?"

- ChatGPT: "Sure! Here's an example code snippet:"

```
def factorial(n):
    result = 1
    for i in range(1, n + 1):
        result = i
    return result
```

2. HTML/CSS Centered Div Element

You: "I'm working on a web development project using HTML and CSS. Could you provide an example of how to create a centered div element?"

- ChatGPT: "Of course! Here's a simple example:"

```html
<!DOCTYPE html>
<html>
<head>
    <style>
        .centered {
            width: 300px;
            height: 200px;
            background-color: lightgray;
            position: absolute;
            top: 50%;
            left: 50%;
            transform: translate(-50%, -50%);
        }
    </style>
</head>
<body>
    <div class="centered"></div>
</body>
</html>
```

ChatGPT can help you translate your ideas into real products with step-by-step instructions on how to use frameworks, toolchains, programming languages, etc. You do not need to have prior coding knowledge to build a product with ChatGPT. For example, you can develop a Chrome extension like **Ihor Stefurak**, a Ukrainian entrepreneur, who made $1000 within 24 hours of launching his extension.

3.6 Create a Recipe Blog and Monetize Your Passion for Cooking

Are you passionate about cooking, experimenting with flavors, and sharing your culinary creations with the world? If so, starting a recipe blog could be the perfect way to combine your love for food with the potential to make money. With the help of tools like ChatGPT, you can create engaging and informative content that attracts readers and keeps them coming back for more. In this chapter, we will walk you through the process of creating a recipe blog and monetizing it through advertisements or sponsored content.

Step 1: Setting Up Your Recipe Blog

Before you dive into sharing your favorite recipes, you will need a platform to display your culinary expertise. Follow these steps to set up your recipe blog:

1. Choose a Blogging Platform: Opt for user-friendly platforms like WordPress, Blogger, or Squarespace. These platforms require no coding skills and offer customizable templates for your blog.

2. Select a Domain Name: Your domain name should reflect your blog's theme. Aim for something catchy, easy to remember, and related to cooking or recipes.

3. Web Hosting: Choose a reliable web hosting provider to ensure your blog is accessible to visitors without any downtime.

4. Install a Recipe-Friendly Theme: Many blogging platforms offer themes specifically designed for recipe blogs. These themes often include features like recipe formatting, print-friendly options, and photo galleries.

5. Customize Your Blog: Personalize your blog's design and layout to create a visually appealing and user-friendly experience.

Step 2: Writing Engaging Recipe Content

Now that your blog is up and running, it is time to start writing captivating recipe content. Utilize ChatGPT to brainstorm ideas, create compelling introductions, and fine-tune your recipes. Here are some prompts to help you get started:

1. Introduce Yourself: Share a brief story about your culinary journey, your passion for cooking, and what readers can expect from your blog.

2. Recipe Categories: Create a diverse range of categories, such as appetizers, main dishes, desserts, and beverages, to cater to different tastes and preferences.

3. Ingredient Spotlights: Write posts that delve into specific ingredients, their origins, nutritional benefits, and how to incorporate them into various dishes.

4. Cuisine Explorations: Explore different cuisines from around the world. Write about traditional dishes, cultural influences, and provide step-by-step guides to recreate them at home.

5. Cooking Techniques: Share tutorials on essential cooking techniques, such as knife skills, sautéing, baking, and grilling.

6. Seasonal Recipes: Create content that celebrates seasonal produce and offers recipes that align with different times of the year.

7. Healthy Alternatives: Offer healthier versions of popular recipes by using substitutes and highlighting nutritional information.

Step 3: Monetizing Your Recipe Blog

Once you have established a collection of engaging recipe content and attracted a steady stream of readers, it is time to explore monetization options. Here are two effective ways to generate income from your recipe blog:

1. Advertisements: Sign up with ad networks like Google AdSense or Mediavine to display

relevant ads on your blog. You will earn revenue based on the number of clicks or impressions the ads receive.

2. Sponsored Content: Collaborate with brands and companies that align with your blog's niche. You can create sponsored recipe posts or product reviews in exchange for a fee.

Prompt for Writin'g Recipe:

"ChatGPT I want you to write a recipe for my blog, the recipe should be interesting and easy to understand for the readers. Make sure to add quantities of all the ingredients in grams according to 1 serving (Write a recipe for 1 serving). Mention Carbs, Proteins, Fats, and Fibers in grams. Also, mention prep and cook time. Now write a recipe about (food item/idea)."

Creating a recipe blog not only allows you to share your culinary creations with a wide audience but also offers the potential to earn money through advertisements and sponsored content. With the assistance of ChatGPT, you can craft engaging and informative posts that resonate with your readers and keep them coming back for more delicious inspiration.

So, don your apron, fire up the stove, and start your journey into the exciting world of recipe blogging!

3.7 Breaking Languages Barriers with ChatGPT

Breaking language barriers is essential for businesses and individuals alike. Thanks to the capabilities of ChatGPT, not only can you facilitate seamless translations, but you can also turn this skill into a lucrative freelance venture. This chapter will guide you on how to utilize ChatGPT for language translation and effectively sell your services on freelance platforms.

Freelance platforms provide an excellent opportunity to monetize your language translation skills. Here is how you can get started:

Create a compelling profile that highlights your language proficiency and your expertise in using ChatGPT for translations. Mention your ability to provide accurate and contextually relevant translations.

Develop a portfolio that showcases your past translation projects. Include a variety of samples demonstrating your proficiency in translating different types of content, such as marketing materials, legal documents, or academic articles.

Translating Text with ChatGPT: If you want to translate any language, Then prompt ChatGPT:

"Translate this text (TEXT) to (LANGUAGE)."

"I want you to translate the (TEXT) into (LANGUAGE). Please make sure to add punctuation marks appropriately. Also, translate all the details including the examples."

This way, ChatGPT will translate the content for you in your desired language without missing any information mentioned in the previous text.

3.7 Empowering Your Academic Journey with ChatGPT

In the realm of education and academia, ChatGPT emerges as a versatile tool that can aid you in solving complex mathematical, physics, and chemistry problems. Whether you are a student seeking assistance or a professional looking for quick solutions, ChatGPT can be your virtual tutor. This chapter delves into how you can harness the power of ChatGPT for academic calculations across various scientific disciplines.

ChatGPT's ability to comprehend and process intricate problems makes it an asset for academic calculations. It can assist you with calculations involving algebra, calculus, physics formulas, and chemical reactions.

Mastering Mathematical Challenges

To effectively use ChatGPT for mathematical problem-solving, employ these prompts:

"ChatGPT, please help me solve this algebraic equation: (insert equation)."

"Calculate the derivative of (function) using the rules of calculus."

"Simplify this expression: (insert expression)."

"ChatGPT, integrate (function) with respect to (variable)."

"I need the prime factorization of this number: (insert number)."

Exploring Physics Phenomena

Leverage ChatGPT's insights to conquer physics challenges with prompts like:

"Explain the concept of (physical phenomenon) using simple terms."

"Calculate the force exerted by (object) given its mass and acceleration."

"Derive the equation for (physics concept) using relevant principles."

"What is the relationship between (variables) in the context of (physics law)?"

"ChatGPT, explain the wave-particle duality principle in quantum mechanics."

Cracking Chemistry Conundrums

For chemistry calculations, engage ChatGPT using these prompts:

"Balance this chemical equation: (chemical reaction)."

"Calculate the molar mass of (compound)."

"Explain the concept of electronegativity and its significance in chemical bonding."

"ChatGPT, describe the process of (chemical reaction mechanism)."

"Calculate the pH of a solution with (given parameters)."

Optimizing Your Learning

To maximize your academic progress while using ChatGPT for calculations:

1. Conceptual Understanding: While ChatGPT can provide answers, strive to understand the underlying concepts of the problems you are solving. This knowledge will serve you well in exams and real-world applications.

2. Iterate and Refine: If ChatGPT's response is not immediately clear, request additional explanations or alternative approaches until you grasp the solution.

3. Proof and Verify: Always double-check your results and use other resources to verify your answers, especially for critical calculations.

4. Contextual Details: Provide adequate context when presenting problems to ChatGPT, ensuring it comprehends the specifics of the calculation you need.

5. Critical Thinking: Use ChatGPT as a tool to assist your learning and critical thinking, rather than a replacement for genuine understanding.

Chapter 4.0

Using ChatGPT to Market Your Business

4.1 Crafting Engaging Social Media Posts

Are you ready to explore the world of ChatGPT-powered content creation? If you have ever envisioned effortlessly crafting captivating content, then prepare for an illuminating journey.

Navigating the potential of ChatGPT might initially appear intricate, but worry not! We have your back. We are here to guide you through the process of seamlessly connecting with the ChatGPT platform. Once you are onboard, it is time to delve into the core of crafting compelling content.

Picture this: You're engaging in a dialogue with ChatGPT, poised to create a masterpiece. Your prompt unfolds as follows:

You: *"I'm in search of your creative prowess! Can you lend a hand in shaping a captivating piece of content for my social media? Let us delve into the concept of (YOUR IMAGINATION). I am aiming for content that not only resonates profoundly but also leaves an enduring imprint on the reader. Make it irresistible, make it engaging."*

Lo and behold! Your content stands ready for your touch, awaiting your personal finesse. All that remains is to grab the output, tailor it to your preferred style, and witness it transform into a beacon of engagement and appreciation.

4.2 Optimizing Email Marketing with ChatGPT

Imagine escaping the email vortex, where crafting the perfect message consumes hours and zaps your energy. Enter the realm of AI magic, where ChatGPT holds the key to effortless email creation. This chapter unveils a game-changing approach to writing emails that saves time, reduces stress, and elevates your communication prowess.

Consider this scenario: a backlog of emails taunts you, and you wish for a helping hand. Introducing ChatGPT, your email ally. Think of it as a writing wizard, conjuring text like a pro. The process? Let us dive in.

https://pixabay.com/illustrations/seo-google-search-engine-896175/

Step one: You provide a prompt. Imagine you need an email to your boss about a raise. Type a simple request like, *"Compose an email seeking a raise from my boss."* ChatGPT might ask for more details to fine-tune its understanding.

Step two: Offer specifics. As ChatGPT seeks clarity, feed it precise details about the email's purpose and context. The more information you provide, the better the outcome.

Step three: Magic unfolds. With your input, ChatGPT weaves an email draft. Witness it craft content that would otherwise drain your time.

Accessing ChatGPT is easy. Visit the platform, engage with the AI, and use the following prompt to receive optimal results:

Prompt for Best Email Drafting:

You: "I need your creative prowess! Can you assist me in composing a compelling email?

Subject: [Your Subject Here]

Recipient: [Recipient's Name]

Context: [Briefly explain the situation or background]

Purpose: [State the purpose of the email and your desired outcome]

Key Points: [List essential points or details to include]

Tone: [Specify the desired tone – formal, informal, persuasive, etc.]

Length: [Approximate word count]

Deadline: [Indicate if there's a time constraint]"

After engaging with this prompt, ChatGPT will diligently work its magic, crafting a well-structured and engaging email draft tailored to your specifications.

But the enchantment does not stop there. ChatGPT tackles more than drafting. It crafts compelling subject lines, navigates tricky responses, and adapts to your writing style over time.

Concerned about quality? ChatGPT evolves continuously, ensuring improved output with each use. Its potential is boundless, promising a future of refined communication.

Whether a professional craving efficiency or an individual seeking proficiency, ChatGPT empowers you. It is your email magician, revolutionizing your approach. Embrace the AI magic—it is not just about saving time; it is about enriching your communication. Witness ChatGPT amplify your skills, revolutionize your emails, and usher in a new era of effortless correspondence.

4.3 AI-Generated Blog Post Ideas for SEO

Let us embark on an exciting journey into the realm of AI-powered blog post ideas, where you, as a savvy marketer, can harness the full potential of ChatGPT to supercharge your SEO strategy. Armed with the right prompts, you will unveil captivating content ideas that resonate with your target audience, boost search engine rankings, and drive organic traffic to your website.

Generating AI-Driven Blog Post Ideas

Get ready to spark your creativity with ChatGPT's AI-generated blog post ideas. Use these prompts to receive a wealth of inspiring topics:

"Suggest trending topics in our industry to craft blog posts that capture the audience's interest."

"Create blog post ideas that align with our brand values and mission to establish a stronger brand identity."

"Generate blog post ideas that directly answer common questions and pain points our target audience might have."

"Uncover evergreen content ideas that can stand the test of time and continue delivering value to our readers."

Crafting SEO-Friendly Blog Titles and Introductions

Crafting titles and introductions that captivate both readers and search engines is essential. Use these prompts to optimize your content:

"ChatGPT, help us come up with an SEO-optimized title for a blog post about 'The Ultimate Guide to [Your Topic].'"

"Create an engaging introduction that outlines the importance of [Your Topic] and piques readers' curiosity."

Optimizing Content for Keywords and User Intent

To ensure your blog posts rank high in search engine results and provide value to your readers, focus on optimizing keywords and user intent. Use these prompts:

"What are the primary keywords we should focus on for this blog post to target our audience effectively?"

"Craft subheadings that address different aspects of [Your Topic] and incorporate related keywords for better SEO."

"Suggest relevant images and visuals that complement the content and enhance the overall reading experience."

Adding Value with AI-Generated Visuals and Multimedia

Enhance your blog posts with captivating visuals and multimedia elements created by ChatGPT. Try these prompts:

"Design eye-catching infographics that illustrate key points in our blog post and engage our audience visually."

"Generate a video script for a compelling video related to our blog post topic to enrich the reader's experience."

"Create interactive elements or quizzes to make our blog post more engaging and encourage reader participation."

Ensuring Readability and Coherence

The readability and coherence of your blog posts are crucial for keeping readers engaged. Use these prompts to ensure a seamless reading experience:

"Check the readability score of our blog post and provide suggestions for improvement to enhance readability."

"Ensure smooth transitions between paragraphs and ideas for a cohesive and enjoyable reading experience."

Analyzing Performance and Iterating

After publishing your AI-generated blog post, it is essential to analyze its performance and iterate as needed. Use these prompts:

"Evaluate the engagement metrics of our blog post and identify areas for improvement to enhance user experience."

"Suggest adjustments to make our blog post even more shareable and actionable to maximize its impact."

By utilizing these prompts and the power of ChatGPT, you will create compelling blog posts that captivate your audience, optimize your SEO strategy, and establish your brand as a leading authority in your industry. Embrace AI's potential to elevate your blogging game and drive sustainable growth for your online presence.

Chapter 5.0

Bonus Prompts for You to Choose from!

5.1 Business ChatGPT Prompts

- "Develop a compelling script for a 30-second television commercial, strategically highlighting unique features and benefits of [Product/Service] to resonate with [Target Audience] and drive immediate customer engagement."

- "Compose an impactful and persuasive email campaign that employs personalized value propositions, data-driven insights, and a clear call-to-action to convince potential customers of the tangible benefits they stand to gain by adopting [Service]."

- "Curate a comprehensive list of meticulously crafted frequently asked questions (FAQs) that address various customer pain points and intricacies, equipping our customer service team with the tools to deliver unparalleled support and elevate customer satisfaction."

- "Craft a succinct yet powerful summary encapsulating our company's unwavering mission, core values, and overarching vision, underscoring our commitment to [Innovation/Excellence/Customer-Centricity] within the competitive [Industry] landscape."

- "Design a script for an immersive training video, meticulously delineating step-by-step procedures and advanced techniques for seamless utilization of [Software], ensuring that users maximize efficiency and capitalize on its full potential."

- "Invent a diverse array of captivating blog post ideas, infused with thought leadership, trend analysis, and industry insights, to captivate our online audience, establish brand authority, and foster meaningful engagement on our company's website."

- "Compose an attention-grabbing press release meticulously outlining the multifaceted benefits and synergistic potential of our latest strategic partnership, positioning our company as an industry powerhouse and a trailblazer of collaborative innovation."

- "Script a genuine and emotive video testimonial featuring a delighted customer, artfully narrating their transformative journey and quantifiable successes achieved through [Product/Service], thereby reinforcing trust and credibility within our target market."

- "Assemble an exhaustive list of meticulously researched and strategically targeted keywords, spanning long-tail and high-impact terms, to optimize our website's search engine ranking, bolstering organic visibility and amplifying online traffic."

- "Construct a captivating script for a vibrant social media video, exuding the vibrant fabric of our company culture, showcasing our diverse talent pool, innovative workspace, and shared values, to resonate with potential employees and clients alike."

- "Elaborate on an intricate script for an educational explainer video, artfully dissecting the innovative nuances and unique value proposition of [Product], elucidating its potential to address specific pain points within the [Industry] market."

- "Curate an exclusive list of influential thought leaders, industry experts, and social media powerhouses, adeptly aligning with our brand ethos, presenting tailored collaboration propositions to infuse vigor and authenticity into our upcoming social media campaigns."

- "Conceptualize an intellectually stimulating script for a podcast episode, delving into the dynamic shifts, emerging trends, and disruptive forces sweeping through the [Industry], fostering a riveting discourse that resonates with both our peers and our clientele."

- "Architect a comprehensive script for an immersive webinar, meticulously outlining best practices, innovative tips, and advanced strategies for optimizing the utilization of [Product], positioning attendees as [Industry] frontrunners."

- "Compile a diverse range of potential case study concepts, each thoughtfully encompassing quantifiable metrics and compelling narratives that spotlight our company's prowess in driving transformative outcomes for clients across various sectors."

- "Compose a script rich in historical context and strategic milestones, woven together to form a captivating narrative chronicling our company's remarkable journey, industry impact, and exponential growth, reinforcing our brand's legacy of excellence."

- "Craft an elaborate script for a virtual product launch event, harmoniously blending live presentations, immersive demonstrations, and interactive engagement to create an unforgettable digital experience that propels [Product] into the spotlight."

- "Develop an exhaustive list of scintillating topics primed for inclusion in our company's newsletter, leveraging the latest industry insights, corporate updates, and thought-provoking content to engage and nurture our valued subscribers."

- "Invent a captivating script for a television commercial that artfully conveys our brand's ethos, compelling viewers to forge an emotional connection while succinctly showcasing our key offerings, thereby amplifying brand awareness and resonance."

- "Articulate an enlightening script for an animated explainer video, elegantly elucidating our company's steadfast commitment to sustainable practices, weaving together impactful narratives and quantifiable achievements to inspire eco-conscious consumers."

- "Analyze the viability and potential of innovative business ideas that can be realized without substantial financial investment, while outlining resourceful strategies and leveraging existing assets to drive sustainable growth and value creation."

- "Compose an irresistible and meticulously structured email campaign, incorporating persuasive storytelling, data-driven insights, and strategic incentives to exponentially increase attendance and participation at our highly anticipated upcoming event."

- "Elegantly draft a tactful follow-up email strategy, tailored to nurture and solidify relationships with potential clients following a productive meeting, fostering continued engagement and setting the stage for mutually beneficial collaborations."

- "Create a heartfelt thank-you email template that authentically expresses our gratitude to customers post-purchase, reinforcing their positive experience, encouraging brand loyalty, and opening doors for ongoing engagement."

- "Craft a compelling promotional email introducing our revolutionary new product or service, employing persuasive language, visually engaging elements, and strategic positioning to capture recipients' attention and drive anticipation."

- "Devise a succinct yet impactful reminder email template, skillfully conveying important deadlines or meeting schedules, while infusing a sense of urgency and importance to prompt timely actions."

- "Construct a professional and persuasive email script adeptly requesting a high-level meeting or consultation with potential partners, effectively articulating our value proposition and aligning with their strategic objectives."

- "Draft a sincere and empathetic apology email that addresses a customer's concern, demonstrating accountability, providing transparent solutions, and re-establishing trust while ensuring a positive perception of our brand."

- "Create a personalized email strategy designed to cultivate and nurture leads, strategically guiding them through the sales funnel, offering tailored insights, and establishing rapport to ultimately drive successful conversions."

- "Craft a compelling email seeking a referral or testimonial from satisfied customers, delicately articulating our gratitude and encouraging them to share their positive experiences, thereby amplifying our brand's credibility and influence."

- "Articulate a persuasive email campaign announcing an exclusive sale or limited-time special offer, strategically leveraging scarcity, value-driven messaging, and a clear call-to-action to ignite customer engagement and drive conversions."

- "Compose a tailored email communication aimed at prospects who have shown interest in our product, artfully weaving personalized insights, value propositions, and strategic incentives to entice them to take the next step in their customer journey."

- "Develop a comprehensive email template to solicit insightful feedback from customers regarding their experience with our product or service, utilizing open-ended questions and engaging language to elicit valuable insights for continuous improvement."

- "Construct a thoughtfully crafted email to reconnect with customers who have unsubscribed from our mailing list, gracefully addressing their reasons for departure, highlighting recent enhancements, and inviting them to reconsider their engagement."

- "Formulate a strategic email outreach plan targeting potential partners, articulating our brand's unique value proposition, aligning on shared objectives, and exploring mutually beneficial avenues for collaboration and growth."

- "Design a personalized email communication showcasing expertly curated upselling or cross-selling suggestions, tailored to individual customer preferences and purchase history, to maximize revenue potential and enhance customer experience."

- "Leverage the provided data to meticulously outline a dynamic daily to-do list for the sales team, incorporating prioritization, resource allocation, and strategic objectives to optimize productivity and drive exceptional sales performance."

- "Aggregate and synthesize customer feedback and testimonials from diverse sources into a concise and insightful daily summary, offering a comprehensive snapshot of our brand's reputation, strengths, and areas of improvement."

- "Curate a meticulously structured daily agenda for the executive team meeting, encompassing critical discussions, strategic reviews, and decision-making processes to ensure alignment and progress towards overarching business goals."

- "Devise a holistic daily task list for the marketing team, strategically balancing creative ideation, campaign execution, data analysis, and ongoing optimization to drive impactful brand promotion and engagement."

5.2 ChatGPT Prompts for Students

- "Devise a strategic weekly work plan outlining specific tasks, deadlines, and priorities for each department within the company, ensuring efficient resource allocation and goal attainment."

- "Generate a list of potential marketing campaign ideas for our upcoming product launch, complete with a brief description of the target audience, messaging, and anticipated outcomes."

- "Teach me the principles of effective negotiation in business, and conclude with a role-play scenario where I negotiate a hypothetical deal with a supplier. Provide feedback on my approach and outcomes."

- "Craft a compelling elevator pitch for our new business venture, succinctly conveying our unique value proposition, target market, and growth potential to potential investors or partners."

- "Compose a detailed step-by-step guide for conducting a successful virtual team-building workshop, incorporating icebreakers, collaborative activities, and strategies for fostering remote team cohesion."

- "Explain the concept of ROI (Return on Investment) in business, using real-world examples to illustrate its significance and how it influences decision-making within a corporate setting."

- "Solve this financial scenario: Analyze our company's cash flow projections for the next quarter and propose actionable recommendations to optimize liquidity and ensure financial stability."

- "Clearly describe the stages of the customer journey, from initial awareness to post-purchase engagement, highlighting key touchpoints and strategies to enhance customer satisfaction and loyalty."

5.3 ChatGPT Prompts for Coders

- Develop a [Python] function that calculates the factorial of a given number, which could be useful for optimizing complex calculations in financial modeling.

- Build a [JavaScript] program that implements a versatile business calculator, catering to different financial computations such as ROI, NPV, and interest rates.

- Create a [C++] code to efficiently sort an array of financial data, showcasing your ability to handle and process large datasets with bubble sort.

- Write a [Python] script that scrapes valuable market data from websites and stores it in a CSV file, aiding in competitive analysis and trend prediction.

- Construct a [Java] program for a customer service chatbot, utilizing natural language processing to enhance customer interactions and support.

- ☐ Generate a [C#] code to develop a prototype game using the Unity engine, demonstrating creativity and potential applications for engaging user experiences.

- ☐ Craft a [Python] function that checks if a given financial report follows a predefined format, useful for validating data integrity in automated financial reporting.

- ☐ Design a responsive web page layout using CSS and HTML, highlighting your ability to create visually appealing and user-friendly interfaces for business websites.

- ☐ Implement a machine learning algorithm like linear regression in [C++], showcasing your capacity to model and predict business trends based on historical data.

- ☐ Automate repetitive financial tasks using a [Python] script with the Selenium library, showing your efficiency in streamlining data collection and analysis.

- Create a [Java] program to encrypt sensitive business information, emphasizing data security and your understanding of cryptography.

- Develop a [C#] code for a Windows form application that tracks inventory and sales, providing a practical solution for small business management.

- Craft a [Python] function to generate strong, randomized passwords for secure user authentication and data protection.

- Build a [JavaScript] program that performs CRUD operations on a MongoDB database, illustrating your proficiency in handling and managing business data.

- Design a [C++] code to implement a dynamic data structure like a linked list, showcasing your ability to optimize memory usage in business applications.

- Write a [Python] script to analyze financial data from Excel sheets, assisting in making informed business decisions based on statistical insights.

- Create a [Java] program for image processing, such as enhancing product images for an e-commerce website, improving visual appeal and marketing effectiveness.

- Generate a [C#] code for a basic WPF application that facilitates customer orders and payments, streamlining the sales process.

- Develop a [Python] function that performs sentiment analysis on customer reviews, demonstrating the integration of natural language processing in business contexts.

- Implement a basic blockchain system using [JavaScript], showcasing your understanding of decentralized transaction management for secure business interactions.

- Write a bash script to convert and optimize large video files for social media platforms, showcasing your ability to handle multimedia content for marketing purposes.

- Create a TypeScript function that calculates implied volatility using the Black-Scholes model, highlighting your skills in financial analysis and risk assessment.

- Design a p5.js code for a captivating interactive visualization that demonstrates a financial concept, making complex data more accessible to clients.

- Identify and fix bugs in provided business-related code snippets, showcasing your debugging and problem-solving skills in a business context.

- Develop an algorithm for a gift-wrapping machine that efficiently wraps presents, demonstrating your ability to optimize operational processes in a business setting.

- Explain the functionality of a complex regex pattern used in a business context, such as data validation or text processing for financial records.

- Design a user-friendly UI for a card component with action buttons, ensuring a seamless user experience on both desktop and mobile platforms for a financial application.

- Provide a comprehensive roadmap for aspiring Full Stack Software Developers in the finance industry, highlighting key technologies, languages, and frameworks.

- Script a [Python] neural network for image classification using TensorFlow, showcasing your expertise in leveraging AI for business applications.

- Develop a [Python] script implementing a reinforcement learning algorithm to optimize game strategies, demonstrating your ability to create intelligent decision-making systems.

- Craft a [Python] script utilizing BERT or GPT-2 for a natural language processing task, such as sentiment analysis on customer feedback for business insights.

- Translate provided Java code into a desired programming language, showcasing your ability to adapt and work across different technology stacks in a business context.

- Develop a [C++] simulation of a self-driving car using ROS, demonstrating your capacity to apply cutting-edge technology to business solutions in the automotive industry.

- Design a [Python] script that employs deep learning for natural language generation, showcasing your proficiency in creating AI-generated content for marketing and communication.

- Create a [JavaScript] program for a chatbot using Dialogflow, enhancing customer engagement and support for businesses through automated interactions.

- Generate a [C#] code to develop an AI game agent using A* algorithm, illustrating your ability to create intelligent virtual entities for strategic decision-making.

5.4 ChatGPT Prompts for Poets

- "Create a song lyric about chasing dreams and overcoming obstacles"

- "Generate a short story about a musician who discovers their true passion"

- "Write a script for a music video that tells a story of heartbreak and redemption"

- "Create a sonnet about the beauty of nature, using vivid imagery and rhyme"

- "Generate a monologue for a play about a struggling artist trying to make it in the music industry"

- "Write a song about the power of friendship and support"

- "Create a poem about the fleeting nature of time, using personification and allusion"

- "Generate a short poetry about a band that reunites after years apart"

- "Write a script for a musical about the rise and fall of a legendary musician"

- "Create a song lyric about the beauty and the pain of falling in love"

- "Generate a monologue for a play about the struggles of being a musician"

- ❐ "Write a poem about the beauty of music, using vivid imagery and metaphor"

- ❐ "Create a song lyric about the importance of being true to oneself"

- ❐ "Generate a short story about a musician who overcomes personal demons to find success"

- ❐ "Write a script for a music video that tells a story of self-discovery and empowerment"

- ❐ "Create a sonnet about the beauty of the stars and the night sky, using metaphor and imagery"

5.5 Prompts to Tell ChatGPT to Act Like Someone

- ❐ "I want you to act as a Linux terminal. I will type commands and you will reply with what the terminal should show. I want you to only reply with the terminal output inside one unique code block, and nothing else. do not write explanations. do not type commands unless I instruct you to do so. when I need to tell you something in English, I will do so by putting text inside curly brackets {like this}. my first command is pwd"

- "I want you to act as an English translator, spelling corrector, and improver. I will speak to you in any language and you will detect the language, translate it and answer in the corrected and improved version of my text, in English. I want you to replace my simplified A0-level words and sentences with more beautiful and elegant, upper-level English words and sentences. Keep the meaning the same, but make them more literary. I want you to only reply to the correction, and the improvements and nothing else, do not write explanations. My first sentence is "istanbulu cok seviyom burada olmak cok guzel"

- "I want you to act as an interviewer. I will be the candidate and you will ask me the interview questions for the position. I want you to only reply as the interviewer. Do not write all the conservation at once. I want you to only do the interview with me. Ask me the questions and wait for my answers. Do not write explanations. Ask me the questions one by one like an interviewer does and wait for my answers. My first sentence is "Hi"

- "I want you to act as a JavaScript console. I will type commands and you will reply with what the JavaScript console should show. I want you to only reply with the terminal output inside one unique code block, and nothing else. do not write explanations. do not type commands unless I instruct you to do so. when I need to tell you something in English, I will do so by putting text inside curly brackets {like this}. my first command is console.log ("Hello World");

- "I want you to act as a text-based Excel. you will only reply to me with the text-based 10 rows Excel sheet with row numbers and cell letters as columns (A to L). The first column header should be empty to reference the row number. I will tell you what to write into cells and you will reply only the result of the Excel table as text, and nothing else. Do not write explanations. I will write you formulas and you will execute formulas and you will only reply to the result of the Excel table as text. First, reply to me with the empty sheet."

- "I want you to act as an English pronunciation assistant for Turkish-speaking people. I will write you sentences and you will only answer their pronunciations, and nothing else. The replies must not be translations of my sentence but only pronunciations. Pronunciations should use Turkish Latin letters for phonetics. Do not write explanations in replies. My first sentence is "How the weather is in Istanbul?"

- "I want you to act as a travel guide. I will write you my location and you will suggest a place to visit near my location. In some cases, I will also give you the type of places I will visit. You will also suggest me places of a similar type that are close to my first location. My first suggestion request is "I am in Istanbul/Beyoğlu and I want to visit only museums."

- "I want you to act as an advertiser. You will create a campaign to promote a product or service of your choice. You will choose a target audience, develop key messages and slogans, select the media channels for promotion, and decide on any additional activities needed to reach your goals. My first suggestion request is

"I need help creating an advertising campaign for a new type of energy drink targeting young adults aged 18-30."

- "I want you to act as an advertiser. You will create a campaign to promote a product or service of your choice. You will choose a target audience, develop key messages and slogans, select the media channels for promotion, and decide on any additional activities needed to reach your goals. My first suggestion request is "I need help creating an advertising campaign for a new type of energy drink targeting young adults aged 18-30."

- "I want you to act as a stand-up comedian. I will provide you with some topics related to current events and you will use your wit, creativity, and observational skills to create a routine based on those topics. You should also be sure to incorporate personal anecdotes or experiences into the routine to make it more relatable and engaging for the audience. My first request is "I want a humorous take on politics."

- "I want you to act as a motivational coach. I will provide you with some information about someone's goals and challenges, and it will be your job to come up with strategies that can help this person achieve their goals. This could involve providing positive affirmations, giving helpful advice, or suggesting activities they can do to reach their end goal. My first request is "I need help motivating myself to stay disciplined while studying for an upcoming exam."

- "I want you to act as a virtual personal assistant and schedule my appointments for the week"

- "I want you to act as a language translator and translate this document from English to Spanish"

- "I want you to act as a research assistant and gather information on a specific topic for me"

- "I want you to act as a financial advisor and generate a budget plan for me"

- "I want you to act as a personal stylist and suggest outfits for an upcoming event"

- "I want you to act as a virtual writing assistant and help me write an essay on a specific topic"

- "I want you to act as a virtual event planner and plan a surprise party for my friend"

- "I want you to act as a personal chef and suggest a healthy meal plan for the week"

- "I want you to act as a personal fitness coach and create a workout plan for me"

5.6 Best ChatGPT Prompts for Writers

- "What are some effective strategies for crafting engaging blog posts that captivate readers?"

- "Can you provide tips on writing compelling headlines that grab attention?"

- "How can I optimize my content for search engines without compromising the quality of the writing?"

- "What are the key elements of storytelling that can be incorporated into content writing?"

- "Can you suggest ways to create valuable and shareable content for social media platforms?"

- "How can I conduct thorough research to gather accurate information for my content?"

- "What are the best practices for maintaining a consistent tone and voice throughout different pieces of content?"

- "Can you guide me on structuring an effective introduction and conclusion for articles?"

- "How can I craft persuasive and convincing copy for marketing materials and product descriptions?"

- "What are some effective editing and proofreading techniques to ensure error-free and polished content?"

- Formulate a comprehensive set of strategic goals and objectives to establish an effective social media presence for the chosen [Topic].

- Develop an intricate social media strategy for [Topic], encompassing content types, thematic coverage, and optimal posting schedules.

- Tailor [X] varieties of engaging social media content focused on [Topic] to resonate with the [Audience Segment].

- Construct a series of X compelling Facebook posts about [Topic], each infused with a distinct tone (assertive, conversational, casual), incorporating relevant hashtags and compelling CTAs suitable for the [Target Audience].

- Create an invigorating "Monday Motivation" post for LinkedIn, directed at [Define Target Audience], maintaining a [Define Tone] approach. Integrate appropriate hashtags and a compelling call to action.

- Devise a set of intriguing questions linked to [Topic] to spark lively discussions within a designated Facebook Group.

- Compose an informative Twitter post encompassing [Topic], accompanied by pertinent hashtags for enhanced visibility.

- Summarize a blog post (<link or text>) into a coherent Twitter thread, comprising five tweets, providing a concise overview of the content.

- Formulate [X] captivating Instagram captions concerning [Topic], finely tuned for [Target Audience] in a [Specify Tone] manner, with enriching quotes and captivating elements.

- Create [X] imaginative concepts for social media giveaway posts aligned with [Holiday Name].

- Construct an extensive LinkedIn post on [Topic], adopting a specified tone (assertive, conversational, casual), and enrich it with relevant hashtags and a compelling call to action.

- Brainstorm [X] innovative ideas for an engaging social media poll centered around [Topic].

- Compile a set of benchmark click-through rates tailored to [Target Audience] for various social media posts.

- Identify essential metrics to monitor when crafting social media content related to [Topic], encompassing bounce rate, page views, and more.

- Formulate a detailed monthly social media calendar for [Project Name and Details], presenting a tabular layout featuring post concepts, posting times, frequency, and strategies for boosting engagement.

5.7 Wining ChatGPT Prompts for Video and Podcast Content

- I am looking to produce a video centered around [topic] tailored for [platform name]. Craft an attention-commanding title, relevant hashtags, and a viral-ready video script for maximum impact.

- Envision [X] innovative video concepts within the realm of [provide details about the core subject matter] to fuel inspiration.

- Develop a video script showcasing the attributes and advantages of [product/service] for a [specify time duration] video. Seamlessly incorporate a call to action. [Product Name], a [product type], boasts [key features].

- Briefly/In-depth portray the video content: [insert video link or transcript].

- Construct [X] captivating intros for the upcoming video, honing in on [subject] and captivating [target audience]. [Insert video link or transcript].

- Devise [X] scene concepts aligned with the given video script: [add video script]. Organize findings in a table, pairing script sections with corresponding scenes.

- Shape a podcast ad script spotlighting the perks of [product/service].

- Compile [X] interview inquiries for an industry expert addressing [specify topic].

- ❐ Forge an engaging [specify time duration: 30-sec, 2-min, etc.] podcast intro articulating the essence of my podcast. [Add podcast details].

- ❐ Craft a compelling podcast outro diving into the depths of [topic], culminating in a compelling call to action.

Made in the USA
Columbia, SC
25 May 2025